MENDED

Also by Anna White

Soul Rest: Retreating to the Heart of Life

You are Irreplaceable. You are Loved. You Matter: Heart Affirmations for my Sister in the Dark

Decoding Etsy SEO

The Light and Fallen

MENDED

THOUGHTS ON
FEAR, LOVE, AND LEAPS OF FAITH

ANNA WHITE

(c) 2014 by Anna White

All rights reserved. No portion of this book may be reproduced in any form without permission in writing from the author, except in the case of brief quotations embodied in critical articles or reviews.

For permissions requests contact the author at anna@2dayichoose.com.

All Scripture quotations are taken from *The Message*. Copyright (c) 1993, 1994, 1995, 1996, 2000, 2001, 2002. Used by permission of NavPress Publishing Group.

Cover Design: Anna White/2dayIchoose

Author Photo: Heather Kelley Photography

First Printing: March, 2014

Printed in the United States of America

First Edition: March, 2014

For my husband, whose love showed me it is possible to be both broken and beautiful.

CONTENTS

Mended..1

Circle Back..4

Thanksgiving...11

A Letter to Myself...15

We Are the Others..18

What Love Looks Like.......................................22

Let it All In..25

Worn..27

Run..31

To Oldest, on her 4th Birthday........................34

This is Why I Practice.......................................37

Foreboding Joy 1..41

Love is Forever Tries...45

Grieve..48

Write What You Know.....................................52

Fear is not from God...55

More God than You Can Handle....................59

At Last I Say Thank You...................................61

Thank You Again...67

Scarcity...70

Helen..77

Keystones...77

Thoughts on Staying after Eleven Years Together..........80

Burn...85

Mothers..89

Beginning of the End...93

Light a Candle Against the Dark........................96

Struggle..100

Thank You for your Gift....................................105

Thin Places..108

To a Sister at Christmas....................................111

The Thick Darkness Where God Was..............114

Surrender...117

Foreboding Joy 2...120

Hello Hurricane...123

Shutting Up my Monkey Mind........................126

Shining All the Way Down..............................130

What I Want my Kids to Know.......................133

MENDED

I attended a counseling conference recently themed *Transformation through Adversity*. I love that. It reaches right into a little place in my heart hand gives it a squeeze. "God yes," my heart says. "Let's do that.

One of the speakers talked about the Japanese art of kintsugi, the art of beautiful repair. "When beautiful things are broken," she said, "the cracks can't be vanished. The breaks are there, and there's no hiding them. Instead each of those breaks, each chip, is filled with gold resin, smoothed down, and made whole again. The broken thing is made even more beautiful."

I walked into counseling months ago, sat down and said, "I'm here because I'm broken." There was no question if I was broken; I knew it. I felt the breaks all the way to my bones.

I woke up each morning and wondered if I would be alive at the end of the day.

I had panic attacks driving to work.

I felt like something was sitting on my chest and stealing all my fresh air.

I was spinning apart, a dark core of gravity pulling me down, down, down.

I was never good enough.

I said, "I'm broken, but I have to learn how to live. I feel stuck together with scotch tape, like after any breath everything could come apart. If it does, if it all comes undone, I think I'll fall down and never rise again."

A lot has happened since then. It is amazing, this journey. The people that we find, and that find us; the hands that show up to hold us.

I am able to sit here today and write words that I thought I never could. *I am enough.*

I do not have to earn it. I can't work my way toward it. I'm not better than you for knowing it.

I am enough.

And so are you.

The most amazing thing is that all my sorrows, all of my darkest moments, are becoming my gifts. The stories in this book are my lifelines to throw out into the stormy sea, words I can use to float someone else just a little longer. They let me say I've been there and mean it.

I know what it's like to sleep in fear, to starve myself to be worthy, to be ashamed of my voice, to want to sleep forever. To question why I deserve to live. I speak, not from a place of professional skill and education. I speak from the other end of the tunnel.

Being broken isn't the worst thing. We can be mended and put together again. We don't have to be ashamed of our past. We can embrace the history that gives us value and see our cracks as beautiful. We can be better than new.

Anna White

"I ask you right here please to agree with me that a scar is never ugly. That is what the scar makers want us to think. But you and I, we must make an agreement to defy them. We must see all scars as beauty. Because take it from me, a scar does not form on the dying. A scar means, *I survived.*"
Chris Cleave, Little Bee

CIRCLE BACK

I have a fantasy that if I could go somewhere alone for a few days or weeks, I could get clarity on the meaning and purpose of my life. Everything seems possible, would *be* possible, if I could just be alone and quiet and the world would stop spinning.

My husband says this longing for isolation is not a good quality, that if I wanted to be a hermit I should have moved to the West Coast and adopted a lot of cats, not gotten married and had children that demand to be fed several times a day. I can't argue with this. Now I *have* them. His life and mine and theirs are all tangled up together and can't be teased apart.

I feel the pull on the bad days to run away to a brighter or slower or younger place where I could start over. It is less of a wish to leave them than to leave myself, a desire to mold myself into a better version and start over with fewer mistakes and breaks and secrets. I can't stop believing that given the chance to start from scratch I could become something better, but it's too late. If I tried to start over, I'd be ripped apart at the heart.

Fear often wraps around my chest like clinging vines and squeezes the air out of my lungs. It knocks on my door heavy and hard and has been hanging around as long as I can remember. I've had a lot of therapists, so I've had the opportunity to approach my fear in many different ways. I've faced it head on and sideways and tried to tiptoe up behind it. I tried to banish it and numb it and live with it, and then one day (sweet hallelujah!) I lost it.

I realized that I was *okay* with myself. I was quirky and withdrawn and loud, but I *liked* that. I smiled at strangers without thinking they were going to attack me and drag me into their cars. I went to doctors' offices and touched magazines that had been touched by sick people. I baked bread. I stopped worrying so much about what other people thought of me.

It was a brief and glorious summer that lasted until I became a mother. The first night in the hospital with a snuffling baby girl, I learned that my family was not the only thing that had expanded. There was now a whole new world of opportunities for judgment and self-doubt. Was I holding her enough? Too much? Was she getting enough milk? Why was she breathing so loudly?

I've been at the center of a fear/peace/love triangle ever since. It's hard not to be, when the world itself feels so full of things to fear. I rarely turn on the news, and when I do there is always another tragedy or murder or disaster. Every night there is some new heartache, a life broken that was whole the day before. Every night fuels my feelings of uncertainty and doubt.

I look at my beautiful family and feel awash in gratitude, while in the background the *what if* shadow hovers. *What if* tragedy came to us tomorrow? How would I survive if I lost them? Disaster feels not improbable, but near. Every good day feels like a near miss. Mornings are full of tension; I look down the day at all the opportunities for joy, while I wait for the other shoe to drop.

I thought I was ready to write this book a year ago, after almost nine months of frequent and expensive therapy. I had done a lot of soul work and was learning to allow my clenched, controlling fist to slowly open. It is a beautiful and scary thing to sit open-handed and let all your plans float away like dust. I thought God was healing me, searing closed the wounds on my heart so that I could write about my journey out of the dark.

I was wrong. He was showing me the light so on the worst days I could remember that the sun was still out there and that somehow, eventually, I would feel its warmth again.

My story isn't any harder or more dramatic than any of the other millions of hard stories that we mothers share. We have all cried for our hurting children and wished we could take away their pain.

So many of us, more than I ever realized, have angel babies. We all grieve our own losses and our own secret pains, but the fact that we all go through these places doesn't make them hurt less.

Our family was already struggling with some issues at my daughter's daycare. She would come up to me in the evenings and wrap her arms around my calf. "I love you even though I'm bad," she would whisper.

Then one day she didn't want to go inside anymore, because two other children had told her they were going to bring a gun to school and shoot her. She was four. I didn't know what to do to help her. We were just trying to hold on until the end of the school year.

Then I found out I was pregnant, a 7 in 1000 chance. My IUD was surgically removed and I was told the pregnancy should be fine, but it wasn't. I never stopped spotting. I was never sick enough. We found out at eight weeks that there was no heartbeat, but I didn't miscarry until almost two weeks later.

Those were the darkest days.

There is something that feels deeply and fundamentally wrong with sitting in bed and longing to know if your baby is dead. I vacillated between hope and optimism, certain that the heartbeat would be there in a few days, and dread.

I was home alone during the day, and I lay on my side eating and watching *Toddlers and Tiaras* because I wanted to not feel. I have never been a crier, but I would feel water dripping onto my chest and realize that my eyes were weeping, my body grieving without my consent. Finally miscarrying was a horrible relief. I felt wrung out and betrayed by my own broken body.

It was through these days that I most appreciated all the work that I had done the year before, because although I felt like I was unraveling at the seams, I had enough awareness to not switch to my default. My default is to withdraw and to shut down. I don't want to talk or be touched or hugged. I want to sit, alone, with my pain. This time I was able to do something different. I leaned into the grief.

I still couldn't talk, but I texted my friends. I posted what was happening on Facebook. I cried with my husband.

I didn't hide my sorrow, and something amazing happened. Lots of women texted me back and fed me and told me their stories. I felt like I was being carried over the threshold of a sisterhood of loss. I knew I was not walking alone, and that eventually I would bob back up to the surface of the deep, because the women around me showed me what healing looks like.

Mended

Last spring I sat in my doctor's office. Again. I was having stomach pain and I felt like my bones were burning. He's been my doctor for a long time, so he ordered some tests and suggested I start taking antidepressants, which I turned down because I wasn't depressed. He nodded. That's what I always say. The tests came back negative and I started therapy. Again. I am walking familiar paths.

I think this is the essence of life: to be willing to circle back, to fall in deeper, to relearn what I thought I already knew. I must rewalk roads I thought I had already left for good and fight to reconquer what I thought I had already vanquished. The road to the heart is not a long, linear path, but this turning. There is no race or competition, just God and I going deeper, carving a canyon to the soul.

I know the words by memory: Love is patient and kind. Love is not jealous or boastful or proud or rude. It does not demand its own way. It is not irritable, and it keeps no record of being wronged. It does not rejoice about injustice, but rejoices whenever the truth wins out. Love never gives up, never loses faith, is always hopeful, and endures through every circumstance.

If perfect love casts out fear, then perfect love is what I need.

The idea of *practicing* love is deeply appealing to me, because an acceptance of imperfection is built right in. There is an acknowledgment to myself that I am going to mess this up, an understanding that there is room to grow. Each of my failures just affirms the truth that we are all starting over and rising again.

Practicing love pushes me out of my comfort zone and makes me sweaty and clammy and pale. One of the dictionary definitions of love is "a feeling of warm personal attachment or deep affection", but it's hard to feel warmth and affection when I tend to see people as threats to be managed. Acts of love, for me, are leaps of bravery.

They take me out of my head, away from my own interests and my own wants and my own desires for a few seconds, just long enough for me to see again and be reminded of how small the differences between us really are. It is easy to forget that when I let down my walls, good things can come in.

Love has no demand of us but to keep practicing, to do the next hard thing. Love says, *Come dear. Take the next step.* Love lights our darkness. It is forever tries.

Mended

"Where there is ruin, there is hope for a treasure."
Rumi

THANKSGIVING

Thanksgiving Day I wake up early, because the baby wakes up early. She has a runny nose and eyes and doesn't seem to feel well. I start prepping the food and put a whole turkey into the oven at 8 a.m. I'm happy to be in the kitchen cooking. My girls are running around under my feet eating bananas, and I turn on music as I mix and stir. I already feel full.

Hours later, when we all finally sit down together, the girls are beyond ready for lunch and dive right in. The rest of us pause for grace.

We all eat quietly, concentrating. Afterward, we say what we're thankful for: family, warmth, and food to eat. My daughter says toothpicks and chalk. I say I'm thankful for this moment.

After dinner my dad hugs me and says it was good. It is. All good.

I feel ready to sink into small and still. I have goals set out for the year, and a few big ones rise before me. Where the road will lead I don't know. I try not to even imagine.

No fantasies for me this year. I choose to stay with the now, to be in the lull. I will breathe in deep until I am full. I will whisper the truth that comforts me: *The Lord is my Shepherd. I shall not want.*

Last year, I needed courage. In my One Little Word album I

Mended

listed these synonyms: adventuresomeness, audacity, bravery, dauntlessness, determination, endurance, grit, resolution, spirit. My goal was never to be fearless, that will never be me. As much as I wish it weren't so, I fear. I shake down to my bones whenever I write or speak from a true heart place. I am terrified of being seen and known, and of not being seen and not being known.

My challenge was to let the fear flood in, to feel it and sit with it until the paralysis fades. Then tell my fear, *Hello. I see you. I know you're trying to protect me, but you can't be the boss.*

"I will pursue acts of courage," I wrote last year. "I will leave my comfort zone, and do hard things. When fear and anxiety chase me, I will not go down easy. I will keep moving forward when I fall. I will not make decisions out of fear, or protect myself by living in hiding. I will allow myself to be seen. I will allow myself to be loved."

The roots of courage are heart, the French word coeur and the Latin word cor. It was the Year of the Heart.

Now I sit in the shadow of my new word. Where courage was bold and action, my new word is calm and still. Listen.

Listen to my heart. Listen to the small voice. Listen to the wind. Listen to you.

I don't have any big goals or future dreams or plans. I am focusing on now, the ground right in front of me. I've always let my imagination run free, but now I try to rein it in. Things never turn out the way I imagine, so I am letting them rest. Instead, I am holding just what is in my hand.

Last year my list of intentions was long: to prioritize,

remember, nourish, express gratitude, build relationships, write, grow.

This year I have just one intention: continue.

Every day is a new beginning, the building of a habit. Every action is a step in some direction. There is no pause in living.

Stephen King set a small goal of writing every day, and every day he made an X on the calendar. Then he wrote, one day after another, until the Xs ran across his days. His intention wasn't to write a classic novel or to make money or become famous. None of those things were in his control anyway. His only job was to not break the chain.

This is the only advice I offer you. Pick the small thing, and carry it on. Let it change your life.

Mended

"Ever since happiness heard your name it has been
running through the streets,
trying to find you."
Hafiz

Anna White

A LETTER TO MYSELF FROM THE OTHER SIDE OF THE DARK

Dear Lovely,

I'm thinking about you today, the way things were compared to the way things are. It reminds me of that summer we went sailing. We were learning to sail on a little, single-hulled Sunfish, and when we caught the wind the whole boat leaned toward the water. I panicked. All I felt was falling.

Later, someone took us out on their catamaran with its two hulls set wide apart. When the sails ripped open on that boat we didn't even rock. We caught the wind and skimmed like birds across the skin of the water. We flew.

This is your reminder, dear, that life should not feel like falling. This is your reminder of what was. Don't forget.

You couldn't breathe. You literally could not catch a breath. Living seemed too hard to make sense. You were holding it together because you have steel deep inside, but you were shaking all the time.

You were 95% sure you would be okay, but the other 5% was scary. You weren't quite sure you were safe with yourself, and wondered if one long, dark day the 5% might be the strongest part. You were nervous, just the smallest bit, when you were home alone with your children.

You were sure you were dying. You knew you must be, because you clearly were not made for living. You felt you weren't made to cope with this life.

In the moments you accepted that you weren't dying, you felt so lost. At random moments, in the car, in the store, you would be overcome with disorientation and loss. You would stand in front of a display of bananas and wonder, "What am I doing? Why am I here?"

You felt so disconnected, like your whole life belonged to a stranger.

Here's the truth, Sweetie. Each of those moments was like crashing into a tree. Each of those moments was a harsh and painful warning. There will always be dark days, but when you're smacking into trees every week, every day, then you're in the woods. And the woods are not the place for you to be. You've been lost there before. Once you're in there, it's too dark to find your own way out.

Don't forget how dark the woods can be when you're feeling good again. Don't doubt that the trees are real.

When you start to feel out of control, stop. Breathe.

If you feel like you're in that little Sunfish, clinging to the mast for dear life and hoping not to drown, maybe it's time for help. There's no shame in that. We all need someone to help steer sometimes, so we can stop being afraid and feel the wind on our faces.

"We cannot cure the world of sorrows,
but we can choose to live in joy."
Joseph Campbell

WE ARE THE OTHERS

I was called a so-called Christian a few weeks ago because of my political views. This bothered me deeply, because it strikes right into one of my oldest doubts.

I grew up believing Christians didn't just believe in Jesus. To be saved, people had to look and speak a certain way. They followed a long list of *nots* to ensure their holiness. They fit the mold. They followed the rules.

I tried so hard, because I wanted to be like everyone else. I wanted God to love me, and I wanted everyone else to know I was good, but I was always different. That world was black and white, right and wrong, yes or no. There wasn't room for doubt or depression or heartsick broken bleeding. There was no conversation about how cold the floor tiles are when you fall down on them and wait for words that don't come.

I tried to fake my way along, but I knew in my own heart things weren't clear cut. I saw from a gray place, that for me wasn't so much a thin, dangerous line as a vast ocean holding the narrow black and white shores away from one another. I couldn't see myself that differently from *those people*, and it was my secret shame.

If I didn't see the way real Christians did, then what was I?

Last Saturday morning my family and I went to the park to

sketch flowers. The parking lot was full when we arrived, and we discovered that there was a religious freedom rally in the pavilion next to the park. We didn't hear much of what was said since we were off sitting in the ferns, but what we did hear was about gay marriage.

I typed religious freedom into Google when I got home, and pages of articles appeared that linked religious freedom and gay marriage. I read articles that said religious freedom and gay marriage were completely incompatible. I read articles that said religious freedom was being violated by not allowing gay marriage. I read articles about business owners being sued for declining to provide services for gay weddings, and I learned that in the mind of many Christians gay marriage is one of the greatest threats to religious freedom in this country.

As a born and bred Southerner, raised in a part of the country where the highways still cut a swath through the cotton fields, this feels like a tricky subject. I do not believe that truth changes, but it is clear from taking a short view of history that what society perceives as sinful does change. I grew up where blacks and whites were once not allowed to mingle, and where interracial marriage was viewed as an abomination. The civil rights movement brought change with the force of the law behind it, although the community was still violently opposed. Today, I doubt there is any restaurant that would refuse to serve a black couple or to provide flowers or a wedding cake for a mixed race wedding.

More recently, in the aftermath of 9/11 and the ongoing threats of terrorism that seeped into our consciousness, Muslims have faced discrimination and violence that seems resonant of the race violence of the 1960s. As a Christian, the beliefs of a Muslim are very different from mine. There are beliefs that they hold that I feel, personally, are incorrect, and I'm sure they could turn an eye to my lifestyle and say the same. We see in each other levels of difference. If we are bold enough to name it, I think we might call it sin.

Anyone who believes passionately in something, whether it is Jesus or Allah or the Torah or Science, can cast a disparaging eye around at the rest of us. I was taught growing up not to be unequally yoked with unbelievers, to withdraw myself from the sinful 'others'. But we are *all* others. We are all sinners in someone's eyes.

The reality is that most of us don't wear our sins on the outside. I can't look at you and see if you cheated on your spouse yesterday, or gambled until 2a.m., or embezzled money, or lied on your resume. Unless you're part of an ultra-traditional group, I won't know if you're Jewish or Muslim or Pentecostal or Buddhist. This keeps things so simple and clean. I can sell you coffee without knowing I'm helping you sober up or that I'm taking stolen money or that I'm helping your prepare to drive to the abortion clinic. I am unaware, so I have no responsibility.

But what if you told me? Then what?

For me, the answer is nothing. The actions of customers or coworkers or clients or strangers are actions that I have no control over. It is self-centered to think that by refusing to serve coffee or make flowers arrangements or smile I am doing anything but making another person feel bad. I doubt that anyone has a Damascus moment after experiencing discrimination. Most people seem to have shining moments of change after experiencing grace.

Anna White

"There is within each one of us a potential for goodness beyond our imagining; for giving which seeks no reward; for listening without judgment; for loving unconditionally."
Elisabeth Kubler-Ross

WHAT LOVE LOOKS LIKE

A basic reality of life is that we all struggle. We hurt and have hurt other people. We all feel lost sometimes.

This isn't all we are, but it is a part of who we are. The only question I have when I'm with someone is, "Can they admit it? And will they let me admit it too?"

My impulse when I'm hearing about struggle is to go in elbow deep and try to help fix it. I want to hand out books to read and speak insightful words. I want to say, "I've been there. But now I'm not. Now I'm here and doesn't here look much nicer than there? So get over here with me!"

I had a conversation with a friend about the frustration of not being able to fix problems for other people. I told her she had to release those problems, so big and heavy, because throwing herself against them wasn't making them smaller, she was only hurting herself.

"Perhaps," I said, "these sticky, out-of-control problems are there to help us grow."

"I don't want to do that!" she said. "I'm done with that. I want growth to be over!"

I laughed, because I understand. I want to be done too.

Today I am feeling what it really means to weep with those

who mourn and rejoice with those who rejoice. To show love, all heart out on the table, and say, "I'm in this too. I'm there. I will get up beside you in your big armchair of loss and grief and brokenness and sit with you."

I'm having one of those ugly undone moments where I *want* to see through God's eyes, I *want* to live and breathe and die in love, but it's hard. There are so many people mourning and rejoicing, and the idea of letting myself feel that strikes fear in my heart. It hits right at the core of who I am and what I'm for and what I believe is true.

In the face of struggle, I want to be a crutch. I want to drag you down the road with me, whether you're ready or not. It is so much harder to turn around and walk back across the scorched earth of my own pain, to go back into the places I'm so glad to be free of, and sit right down in the mud.

To not say a word, but to offer my hand.

To just sit in the *there* together.

I think that must be what love looks like.

Mended

"The path to our destination is not always a straight one. We go down the wrong road, we get lost, we turn back. Maybe it doesn't matter what road we embark on. Maybe what matters is that we embark."
Barbara Hall

LET IT ALL IN

I've been flying so high, feet off the ground, every breath a little more air in the balloon lifting me higher. My mind is clicking, filled with a lovely avalanche of ideas. I breathe deep and let myself expand. *Embrace it*, I tell myself. It is the joy that balances out the bottom.

Because the bottom is coming. I feel it, like a little dark shadow around the edge of my happy cloud. I am tippy-toe on the edge of the cliff.

Yet I believe, for the first time in a long time, that I am a happy person. I believe there is, at the heart of me, a core of joy.

I know this core is there because of my capacity to fall into the dark.

It is this, the capacity to feel consuming grief and pain and despair, that also allows me to embrace love and joy and beauty with my whole heart. I must let it all in.

Mended

"May you allow the wild beauty of the invisible world to gather you, mind you, and embrace you in belonging."
John O'Donohue

Anna White

WORN

There are a few things: running, meditation, journaling, that would change my life if I really let them. And I want to change, but because it is scary and unknown I avoid it. This is the struggle. Am I brave enough to bring change in?

Yesterday when I was grocery shopping I couldn't stop thinking the words "Expecto Patronum" over and over. The words literally mean "I await a guardian". I breathed them in and out like a heart rhythm, like a song. I am not enough in myself; I can barely make it through buying milk and school supplies. Thank goodness there is a Guardian to come before me and throw off the dark.

I write about the same things over and over again. Death. Uncertainty. Fear. Faith. The hard and fierce goodness of life. I circle around and around.

Why? Am I a prowling tiger looking for the best moment to leap onto the rounded haunch of my fears and rip into them with my teeth, or just an old dog walking around the same pillow trying to work it into a more comfortable shape to press my belly into.

I wrote this poem several months ago. My husband didn't like it. "It sounds like something I've read before," he said. I laughed, because that's what it's about. What is really new?

I'm not along in my circling. We're all in it together, all of us just going around the things that scare us and hoping to wear them down.

WORN

Sometimes I wonder why I think

I can say anything new

about death or pain

or the joy that touches us all

in one way or another.

What is left to say?

My words are used,

worn smooth

by the singing and weeping

of those who came before.

Does my taking them up

wear them down a bit more?

Are they any closer to revealing their truth?

Or is it just me who is worn?

Anna White

"Be realistic. Plan for a miracle."
Osho

RUN

I went running for the first time in weeks, and I was expecting to struggle and flounder and gasp for breath. I started slow, but my legs itched for more. *Run!* They whispered. *Run harder!* So I did. I ran faster and farther and longer than I ever have.

The sun was setting in front of me, the sky changing and falling into dusky purple and pink and orange. I felt strong. I felt whole, 100% there. The scary little part of me that hides in the back closet and threatens to take over if I'm not careful is gone; I think I've worn him down.

I ran and I thought about all the things that I am. I'm a runner who drinks wine. I'm a counselor that wants to be left alone. I'm a Christian that swears. I'm flamboyant, but I want to fit in. I'm a good friend. I'm a bookworm. I'm a mess. I'm selfish. I'm compassionate.

I have a page in my journal dedicated to all the parts of myself, all the contrary, almost opposites that live in me: responsible/impulsive, capable/overwhelmed, safe/damaged. Before, I thought I had to pick, to find a way to be one thing or the other. That until I could get it under control, I was a mismatched stuck together unperson, all damaged and scary, like Sid's toys in Toy Story.

Today, I feel the air in my lungs and I know that is a lie. I am whole. I am complete. All of my secrets and scars and wishes and dreams can live together in this one body without shame, without blame, and without fear. I am all loved, all accepted, and all in service to God. In his eyes, regardless of what I did or didn't do today, I am loved. I am His, so I am enough.

"Tears are prayers too.
They travel to God when we can't speak."
Psalms 56:8

Anna White

TO OLDEST, ON HER 4TH BIRTHDAY

Oh my darling, four at last! You've been waiting to hold up that finger, the pinkie, with anticipation. When daddy and I came in to wake you this morning we sang, "Happy Birthday. Yay!"

You sat up in bed, rubbed your sleepy eyes, and said, "I'm four?" You held out those four fingers and looked at me for confirmation, because it seemed so sudden after all the waiting.

The last year has been one of transitions. You've struggled with hearing no when you want to hear yes. You've responded to requests with, "but I want" and "I just." There have been tears and fits, times where you fell on the floor and kicked for the sheer frustration of wanting something you could not name.

I tell you, my darling, that this is just the beginning. Life is full of thwarted wants and unnamed longings. This is a lesson that must be learned early and often. I am learning still, because I want for you to be happy and free always, to see the world as full of friends to be made, and to believe baby Jesus is a short trip away. My wishes for you are unsayable, feelings outside of words.

You have grown up so much this year. You are tall and full of dancing energy. You love books and sleep with them every night, but you tell me you're too young to read the words. You color in the lines now and write your names at the top of your worksheets.

Mended

    I have mixed feelings about this. I want you to make beautiful pictures, and they do look a lot better when you stay in the lines. And yet I must beg you to draw your own lines. Make your own picture, and make it bright and beautiful. Make the sky purple and the grass pink if you want to, sweet girl, and don't let anyone make you feel less for it. Don't let anyone steal the color from your world.

Anna White

"To love beauty is to see light."
Victor Hugo

Mended

THIS IS WHY I PRACTICE

Normally all it takes is to close my eyes, and I can feel myself drop like a stone, slipping beneath the surface into stillness. These past few days I'm a duck, bobbing on the surface, feet beneath churning things up like crazy, head bobbing under for a quick sip, and then popping back up to paddle, paddle, paddle.

This reminds me why I have daily practices. Not for the days when quiet wraps me up and I feel unshakable. I practice for the days when it doesn't. I practice so when the noise and exhaustion and fear come along, I don't shut down.

Last Thursday was supposed to be my first day back to work, and my sweet husband set the alarm for 4. I went to bed excited, ready to wake early. It would be the first morning that the Christmas decorations were back in the attic and I would be able to return to my quiet place, my corner with my chair and my books and my blanket.

Then I got up in the night, passed out, and woke up bleeding on the floor. Instead of spending my morning in reading and reflection, I lay in a bed in the emergency room.

Yet even while I lay there on those thin, scratchy sheets, I kept thinking, *This is why I practice.*

I could feel the difference it made, because for once I wasn't planning anyone's funeral. I wasn't choked with panic. Even in that moment, with my daughter's boo-bunny held up to the gash in my lip, several hours in and still not seen by the doctor, I told myself, *Be here. Stay with it.*

I felt blessed, because we were able to go to a hospital, and because I didn't break my nose, which the doctor mentioned isn't uncommon for fainters, and because a friend came over at two in the morning to sleep on my couch so we could go to the emergency room. I felt thankful for my husband who was doing his best to take care of me even though he was scared. I felt thankful that my job is not urgent, nor in jeopardy of being lost in my absence.

Many mornings I pop my head into my boss' office and tell her, "Today is going to be a beautiful day." Thursday I looked around that little curtained room, listened to the nurses joking outside the door, and wondered if I'd been saying it wrong. Maybe it's not about having a beautiful day, but about finding beautiful moments. Maybe a whole day is just too much to ask. Because so far, the day was not turning out beautiful, but it was still early and I had a choice.

Mended

I could choose to believe that in each day, in all things, no matter how dark and ugly, there are shards of beauty, if I look for them.

This is why I wake early. This is why I practice.

It is not about striving for a goal, but about falling into acceptance of my flawed brokenness. It is just the daily doing, in spite of this. The beginning again, and again, and again, and again.

Anna White

"One new perception,
one fresh thought,
one act of surrender,
one change of heart,
one leap of faith,
can change your life forever."
Robert Holden

FOREBODING JOY 1

I'm continually amazed at how most people seem to get life. They just seem to do it so well. All of the hard corners and spiky edges don't seem to dig into their soul, the way they do into mine. Personally, I'm impressed when people just manage to get dressed and show up, but society in general expects more than that.

I don't notice what people wear or what car they drive. I don't know where all my various technology bits are, or whether they're updated, or charged, or whatever. I've got all my energy on figuring out where I'm supposed to be, listening when I get there, and not running into any walls or tables or chairs (or cars) along the way.

I've always thought I would die young, because to me, life has always felt really, really hard. I've always secretly felt bad at it. I'm too sensitive and scattered and messy, and all my pieces have never felt all that together. I just assumed God wouldn't throw me down here, all wander-y and confused, and leave me.

Now that I'm actually accepting the fact that I might live a long and healthy life, two things are happening.

First, I'm afraid that now that I want to live, I'll find out I actually am dying of some esoteric disease. Because life is ironic that way. Yes, I know how crazy that sounds. It is what it is. You'll either be the kind of person that gets it, or you won't.

Second, for the first time I'm actually looking into my future as a real, long possibility. Sometimes the days stretch out before me like the yellow brick road to Oz, and other days they stack up, one on top of the other, until I can't see their end, a mountain of weighty gifts.

Then there are days when I imagine the deaths of those I love, imagining how I would deal with the death of my husband or one of my children, and rehearsing what I would say if I got *the call*. It is in my moments of greatest joy that the fear comes slinking in.

I've always thought this was weird and shoved it into the closet with all my other dirty emotional secrets, but <u>Daring Greatly</u> Brene Brown describes exactly this feeling. I'm not alone! This rehearsal of our worst fears creeps into the lives of lots of us, and the name of this shadow is foreboding joy.

Foreboding joy is the uneasy sense that the other shoe is about to drop, the nervous feeling that comes just as we're sinking into happiness, the voice that whispers, "You don't deserve all this love and beauty and goodness." Foreboding joy

Mended

tells me to hold on tight when my heart is longing to let go. It makes me want to slow down, hold back, and play safe, all to maintain the illusion of control.

Foreboding joy manipulates my feelings, but it is a distorted mirror that doesn't show me reality. It robs me of real, fleeting moments of connection and realness and grace.

This morning Fear is trying his best to get his teeth into me. I'm driving to work and I feel the shaking in my blood, working its way from the inside out. Instead of spiraling down, I look up.

I start listing things that I am thankful for: my girls, my husband, ice water, rising sun.

It doesn't lift the fear altogether, but it pushes open my chest a bit, and gives me a little room to breathe.

I hate my doubts and my dark, ugly thoughts. They are born out of my deepest loves and my greatest vulnerabilities, the areas where I cannot be in control.

I name you today, heart fears. I am small, but you are smaller. You will not stop me.

I put my faith in a God that is bigger. You have a voice, fears, and I must listen, but then I will open my heart. I will love you right to death.

Anna White

"We're made for ebb and flow. Just like the ocean. Just like the cycles of the moon. Just like the movement from dark to light to dark again. We were born to shift and be selfish and howl and get messy. We were made to create beauty and to make crazy love and to find the bliss right at the center of our raw, aching parts."
　　　　　　　　　Jeanette Leblanc

Mended

LOVE IS FOREVER TRIES

I am home today with the girls. Husband is out, and they are lying in their beds. We spent the morning working, they and I, doing the art. I sat at one side of the table with paint on my fingers, and they sat on the other side with crayons in their hands.

It was nothing, but at the same time I think if all they remembered from their childhood was today it would be enough. We were together, making beautiful things.

I keep thinking about forever tries. I show the girls in sign language, my right hand moving out in the shape of a Y. "This is forever," I say, and Oldest nods like she understands.

"Forever tribes," she says. "My favorite kind."

It's my favorite too. I love that there's no cutoff where we get labeled and sent off to a home for hopeless, cranky, depressives. Every day is a new chance to listen longer and be braver and love more. We get to try again and again and again.

I don't believe we ever get perfect, but maybe we can get

Anna White

better. If not today, then tomorrow. If not, we still have chances to go. We're not spent out.

I turn on the radio, and I hear:

Settle down, it'll all be clear.

Do not pay mind to the demons they fill you with fear.

The trouble, it might drag you down.

If you're lost you can always be found.

Just know you're not alone

'cause I'm gonna make this place your home.

I hear, and I listen. The shadow is dark and the woods are cold, but they are not endless. No matter how lost you are now, you are not lost forever. You are findable.

Love just keeps on looking.

Love is forever tries.

Mended

"How could our hearts be large enough for
Heaven if they are not large enough for Earth?
The only paradise I know is the one lit by our
everyday sun, the land of difficult love,
shot through with shadow."
Scott Russell Sanders

Anna White

GRIEVE

I can't stop thinking about grief today, about its hard, dangerous landscape full of hidden crevices and sharp drops and slippery rocks: the shadowlands. We all roam there.

Our society has such fences built around grief, about what we should grieve, for whom, for how long and in what ways. There can be such guilt bound up in the ways we find to cross these lands. Is there too much sorrow? Too little? Do I *look* sad enough? Or too sad? Is my weeping making you uncomfortable because it's too raw and ugly?

The griefs that have been hardest for me were the ones I didn't recognize as griefs, because they came in what were supposed to be the best times of my life. No one whispered in my ear that the best times, the ones that change our lives, are woven with the thread of loss.

The day before I got married, I sat across from my mom in the dark booth of a Mexican restaurant and cried. I was so twisted up I couldn't have articulated one specific thing I was crying about. I was crying about the fact that I was getting

Mended

married at all, the crushing expectations about my role as a wife, the foreboding feeling I had that I would fail, and about the life dreams that I was giving up in place of this uncertain future. I cried more, just from the guilt of crying in the first place. I remember my mom sitting across from me not knowing what to do. "Why are you so *torn up*?" she said. "I don't think I felt like this."

It happened again when I found out I was pregnant with my first daughter. I was so excited. We had tried for years to get pregnant, and I remember suspecting and creeping into the bathroom to take my umpteenth pregnancy test. The joy-fear that washed over me when two blue lines appeared instead of one was a tsunami that rearranged my emotional house.

Yet as the months slipped by, a third line appeared, the line of grief. A baby gives you innumerable gifts, but it also takes things away. It takes away your sleep and your ability to pack light and your money and whole continents of your heart. I was happy, so happy, and I didn't know how to hold the happiness and grief together.

Here's what I wish someone had whispered to me: let yourself feel how you feel. Every change leads to a loss. It's okay, even in the midst of joy, to grieve. The grief doesn't diminish the joy. Life is big enough for both.

Then I read these words in Tiny Beautiful Things by Cheryl

Anna White

Strayed about acceptance and acknowledging the loss of the could've been lives that we let slip through our fingers. They are perfect:

"If I could go back in time I'd make the same choice in a snap. And yet, there remains my sister life. All the other things I could have done instead. Who would I have nurtured had I not been nurturing my two children over these past seven years? In what creative and practical forces would my love have been gathered up? What didn't I write because I was catching my children at the bottoms of slides and spotting them as they balanced along the tops of low brick walls and pushing them endlessly in swings? What did I write because I did?

I'll never know, and neither will you of the life you don't choose. We'll only know that whatever that sister life was, it was important and beautiful and not ours. It was the ghost ship that didn't carry us. There's nothing to do but salute it from the shore."

Mended

"The most beautiful people we have known are those who have known defeat, known suffering, known struggle, known loss, and have found their way out of the depths. These persons have an appreciation, a sensitivity, and an understanding of life that fills them with compassion, gentleness, and a deep loving concern. Beautiful people do not just happen."
Elisabeth Kubler-Ross

Anna White

WRITE WHAT YOU KNOW

I hate the advice to write what you know, because I've spent my whole life learning what I don't know. These wide empty places are my 'negative space'. The knowledge of all that is unlearned and unknowable keeps things in perspective.

The more I read, the more I write, and the more I make connections, the wider the ocean of all my unknowing becomes. I'm not ignorant, I'm filled with facts and trivia, yet with all the things that I know there is so little I Know.

Capital K Knowing, that's the Knowing that matters: the sureness of goodness, a grasp of faith, a belief in the unfailing chaos of life and the security that out of that chaos, improbably, comes love. This is the Knowing that is slippery, hard to hold onto when I am falling. It's so much easier to grab for the things I know, facts and figures and statistics and rules, but there's no heart in that. There's no healing.

I have to let go of my small knowing and let my weight carry me down into the deep where my heart and soul catch on fire. Rilke wrote, "Things aren't all so tangible and sayable as

Mended

people would usually have us believe; most experiences are unsayable. They happen in a space that no word has ever entered." This is truer than true. How can words convey the vast Knowing waiting to be discovered?

I encourage you to throw away the advice to write what you know. Turn inward; look into the blinding burning of your heart. Close your eyes and see what patterns dance there, what impressions are left by that burning light.

Write that. Use your words to sketch an outline of that place and build a bridge that can carry us both across the dark.

Anna White

"Be who you were created to be,
and you will set the world on fire."
St. Catherine of Sienna

Mended

FEAR IS NOT FROM GOD

I sat in a youth service when I was twelve and heard someone preach that our salvation was spider-web fragile. He said we could sin any moment, maybe not even knowing, and if we should happen to die before we could repent for these sins, then we would go to hell. Worse, if we couldn't stop all this regular old human-naturing, then God might kill someone that we love to get our attention.

I remember sitting on a pew with thirty or forty other kids, my fingertips rubbing over the surface of the orange woven seat cushions. We were all on the left side of the church and the podium was down on the floor, just in front of us. The preacher told a story, he swore it was true, about someone who couldn't "get it together". Their car stalled on a train track and their whole family perished so that this person would see the error of their ways and turn to God. It was a horrible story, and I believed every word.

I've thought about this memory many times over the years. It has colored the way I feel about myself, about others, and about God. I built walls and locked myself down, because I believed everything could be taken away at any moment. Love felt dangerous, because I could never be good enough to deserve it. My love felt destructive. Killer.

Now I know, without a doubt or a question, that this is not real. This is a lie. This is not the God I know.

Even in Jesus' time people wanted to grab onto this type of thinking, that our behavior causes blessing or tragedy, that we can control nature, and God, if we try hard enough. Jesus answered this head-on. "He makes his sun rise on the evil and on the good, and sends rain on the righteous and on the unrighteous" (Matthew 5:45).

In <u>Grace for the Good Girl</u> Emily Freeman writes, "Fear drives, love provides". It was fear that drove me to repent and pray and cry. It was fear that drove me to build up walls and run away. It was fear that made me package all my heart's loves up and hide them for safekeeping.

But fear is not from God.

God wants to take the fears that you and I are holding onto with both hands. He throws them aside, effortless, and then takes our empty hands in His and fills them with his love. He is not a hard driver. He wants to provide.

These words filled my mind and my heart when I opened

Mended

my eyes this morning:

"Father God,

I need you today.

You are the guardian I've waited for.

Today I will let you go before me.

Fight for me. Shelter me beneath the wide umbrella of your grace.

Open my understanding to your will and my eyes to the gifts that surround me.

Draw me back into the light if I start to drift into the dark.

Give me the words to comfort the weary.

Help me speak from your wisdom and act from your love.

Help me see myself the way you do, with compassion and gentleness.

Remind me that my worth comes through you.

Calm my fears, and help me embrace the future with hope.

Anna White

"The world may be broken,
but hope is not crazy."
John Green

Mended

MORE GOD THAN YOU CAN HANDLE

"Aren't everything you have and everything you are sheer gifts from God? So what's the point of all this comparing and competing? You already have all you need. You have more access to God than you can handle." 1 Corinthians 4: 7-8

Today remember this verse, wherever you are, however high or low you feel, and no matter how far from where you want to be.

Everything we have, everything we are, is a gift.

How can we judge and shame ourselves if this is true?

You don't need to change first. You don't need to be better. There is nothing you have to do.

Just as you are, right now, you already have all the access to God you could want, even more than you can handle.

Anna White

"What makes you vulnerable makes you beautiful."
Brene Brown

Mended

AT LAST I SAY THANK YOU

Dear Sister,

I was thinking about you tonight while I was walking in the quiet and looking up at the stars. I thought about you, and how you told me that you were angry. Maybe you still are.

I've been angry too. I was angry with the person who hurt me, a little, but mostly I was angry with God. I was angry because I had done everything I was told He wanted.

And how much He wanted. My whole personality was all wrong, too loud and bright and emotional. I tried to build a facade and want the right things. I was chasing my tail around and around trying to find God, but I just dug myself into a hole in the ground.

My heart was breaking under the weight of this impossible salvation, but I tried. I starved. I cried. Then the darkness found me anyway.

I remember lying in my boyfriend's bed one night. He was in the shower and I was alone in the dark and the Counting

Anna White

Crows were singing Round Here on the radio. I cried slow, hot tears because I was so far from where I wanted to be, and I didn't know quite how I got there. All I knew was that I had failed and failed and failed. I wasn't sure I deserved to keep breathing, stealing life from the beautiful world. I didn't want to die, but I was afraid to live because the only future I saw was filled with more failure.

I prayed my last prayer for many years that night. "God, if you are real," I said, "you are not true. I hurt myself to be who you wanted, and it has only brought me pain. Let's try something new. Please leave me alone."

This happened over ten years ago, and all this time when I've looked back on those years it has been a black hole in my memory. I thought of them as the lost years, all blackness, all pain, all suffering.

The trouble with forgetting is that there were good moments in that time too. All the memories of laughter and love and safety were lost to me, because to remember I had to cross back through the darkness and I was afraid.

The only good thing I could see about that time was that it ended.

But God has been working on me.

A few months ago, for the first time in all these years, I saw

Mended

something good about that time. I was alone then, falling into what I now know was my first round with major depression. I was isolated from my family and my church because I was ashamed that my faith was not enough. I remember standing in front of the closet and crying because getting dressed, the act of picking out underwear and a shirt and pants, was impossible. I lay in the dark and cried because being alive hurt so much and I was so young and there was still so much life to go.

The relationship I was in at this time was painful and toxic and broken. We were both damaged, and yet he loved me in his own way. It was a way I hope to never be loved again, but it was still a form of love. He fed me when I could not eat. He carried me to the shower when I could not bathe. He told me that he could see something pure and shining in the heart of me, a diamond in the rough. For this, I am thankful.

I've had to release my shame about the choices I made. I did my best. All the bad things that happened were real and powerful, but so is this simple truth: I lived.

This is the goodness that I see after all this time. For all the darkness and pain and misery brought down on me, I was kept alive.

I have started to remember again, not the dark things, but the good things that were forgotten. I'm remembering all the way back now. Sometimes I wake up and in that half-dream state, and I hear myself laughing. I think this is what it means to be born again.

I don't know how to end this, except to say that it can happen. I believe therapy helps because it lets us hear ourselves. I believe that we have to be ready to dig and walk back into that darkness with our shoes off, to bleed again, maybe, to get to holy ground. I also know that healing goes beyond therapy.

It started for me in silence.

Last January I started getting up every day. I couldn't pray, so I sat in silence every morning until June. Then I wrote this in my journal:

Jesus. God. One high above me,

I believe in you because I need to believe. I have to hope.

Help me not be a jerk.

When people are around me are loud, give me words of love.

Help me appreciate this moment.

Be with me in this beautiful chaos. Come before me, hand beneath me.

Carry me home.

That was the beginning. I am still not good enough. I am

Mended

still not whole enough. I am still not pure enough. I am still weakness and sharp edges and broken, but He is good and pure and whole, all that I strive for but am not.

Now I wake up every morning and I sit in silence and I choose to believe. I may speak. I may not. I let Him wrap up all my broken in to His grace. He takes me imperfect. This is the great mystery I never knew.

Tonight as I walked home I thought, for the first time, Thank you God for my imperfection. Thank you for my damage and my darkness. If I were perfect how would I see you? You are the starlight shining in the night. Thank you for the night that lets me see it. Thank you, thank you, thank you.

Anna White

"Grace and gratitude belong together
like heaven and earth.
Grace evokes gratitude l
like the voice an echo.
Gratitude follows grace like
thunder follows lightning."
  Barth

Mended

THANK YOU AGAIN

I went to a Christian college, and there was an undercurrent of God as a micro-manager there. As in, "I'm sorry I was late for class, but God made all the lights red. Probably to keep me out of a fatal car accident. So don't mark me tardy, 'kay!"

Personally I see God as more distantly involved, able to intervene, but mostly not. I believe God lets us stumble along, slowly finding our way, and giving us chances to pick each other up.

So when a coincidence happens, I have a hard time knowing what to call it. Serendipity? A lucky happening? A God thing? Grace?

I spent the better part of this morning in quiet stillness. I sat in my chair and read emails and posts I had bookmarked. I read a prompt to write a letter of thanks to myself for showing up this past year, even when (especially when) things were hard, and I did. Because I am so thankful that a fighter part of myself decided to crawl out from under the dark covers and live.

Anna White

Then I thought about Five Minute Fridays and how I enjoy those posts in my blog feed. *Maybe I should do that one day*, I thought. I clicked over to Lisa-Jo's site, and what was the prompt?

Thank YOU.

Once again I feel blown off my feet by life. Life is just so big-small-beautiful-crushingly good. What words are there to say except thank you, thank you, thank you.

Dear Lovely,

I am thankful today for the leaps, jump after jump taken off mountains large and small. You knew, I think, that there was a better way to live. Or maybe not. Maybe you just knew to stay in the cold, thin air was to die. You flung yourself out without seeing which arms would catch you. You were brave enough to change your life.

This is why I am thankful. Because now I see that tears and racing heart and sweaty palms are not only part of the leap, but also of the *before*. It all hurts. To stay freezing, forehead pressed to bathroom floor. To leap into the unknown spaces of yourself. It all hurts, but now when I open my eyes I no longer see blurred black and white tiles. I see only clouds and blue, blue sky.

Mended

"The creative force is rumbling through the cells of every female, a cacophony of ideas, urges, manifestations. It is falling like rain, roaring like a tsunami, boiling like water for afternoon tea. Who we are is what we create-our furies, our despair, our ecstasies become the poems, the novels, the operas and plays that melt a heart, change a mind, stamp a culture with its indelible ink."
Jan Phillips

Anna White

SCARCITY

Sunday morning my daughter and I were having a discussion about whether or not to go to church. I'm a sporadic attender at best, I hear God better alone by the water than in a crowded building. She wanted to go, and I was leaning towards staying home since my husband was sick and we would be going alone.

She immediately came up with a plan: "Daddy can stay here with Sophie," she said, "and you can come with me to Sunday School. That way no one will be alone."

"But I'll have to sit by myself," I said.

"I'll be with you," she argued.

"Only in the car. When we go inside you'll go to your class and I'll have to sit alone."

She reached over and patted my arm with her pudgy hand. "It will be okay," she said. "Your friends will be there, and if they're not, people will be kind."

Mended

How could I argue with that? Into the car we went. She's right, of course. She knows what I forget: that people are kind. I have friends everywhere, existing and waiting to be made. Even if I am alone, God's shadow covers me. I am always sheltered, always wrapped up in love. I am always on the edge of kindness.

My fear of being real, of being seen, paralyzes me into silence. I crave the touch and the connection, but I'm not always brave enough to open my hand and reach out. This is the great challenge: to be seen, accepted, and loved, I must first reveal, offer, and surrender.

I want to share my story, and I want to know yours. I believe with all my heart that sharing our stories, the real, ugly, broken ones, is one of the most powerful things in the world, because to share our story we must first accept it. We must own it. We must stop running from it or shoving it into the corner when company comes over. To share our story is to admit that we've been changed.

I am, in the words of Brene Brown, *couraging* every day. I am practicing. There are so many moments when I have a choice to hide or be my real self.

Even getting dressed is a minefield. Do I wear the slacks and sensible shoes or the beaded dress and leopard print heels? If I choose what I love, there is always a spark of anxiety, the wonder of what 'they' will think.

Anna White

I wore an embossed pendant this week that said, Enough. My boss said, "What have you had enough of? Is this like that JLo movie where you want to beat someone up?"

I said, "No, it's not *had* enough. It about me. I *am* enough."

I felt scared and naked saying out in the open, but I believe it. I want you to believe it too. Can we all say it out loud, even if we're only talking to ourselves? Can we embrace the wanton brazenness of believing we're enough?

Let's all be brave together. Let's tell each other our truths.

Mended

"Compassion isn't about solutions.
It's about giving all the love you've got."
Cheryl Strayed

Anna White

HELEN

When I think about God, I think about my grandmother. She was soft and round and shorter than me. I never doubted that she loved me, or that there was anything I could do to make her love me less. I knew I could disappoint her, but her love was a constant.

When I was younger she would make biscuits and dumplings, cutting them out by hand. She seemed to spend half the day in her small, steamy kitchen. She made pancakes in a cast iron skillet late at night and knew how to broil cheese toast to the perfect level of blackness.

I don't know as much as I would like to about her life. I asked her to tell me stories once and she couldn't grasp why. To her it was hard and uninteresting, better left in the past. She did tell me she rode to church in a horse drawn wagon, and that when she married my grandfather she wore her best dress and the preacher married them after the service.

She loved to travel. I don't think she traveled nearly as much as she would have liked, and I wonder if she regretted

Mended

that. She told me stories in the dark, the same ones over and over.

I don't know who all she touched with her life, or how. I'm not even sure she graduated from high school. I don't know what her heart's dreams were, and if she considered them fulfilled at the end of her life.

She was a worrier. She feared like me.

Some days the big God, the glorious burning, is too much for me. Some days that God is too high to reach. On those days I close my eyes and imagine I'm calling her on our old black rotary phone. I can hear her heavy steps vibrating the floorboards as she moves toward the phone, answering always at the end of the third ring.

I can feel her, me half falling off the arm of her big chair, half pressed up against her softness. "Just do your best," she says. "That's enough. Everything is going to work out fine."

Anna White

"Each morning we are born again.
What we do today is what matters most."
Buddha

Mended

KEYSTONES

I've been thinking about keystone habits, the changes that make the others fall in like dominoes, and for me that is journaling. I often look back at words I've written and barely recognize them as my own. They are truths written down for myself on good days, and they whisper to me from the other side of the dark.

I preach, as Ann Voskamp says, to the one who needs it most. Always myself.

One of my favorite quotes is, "Love understands, and therefore waits." I don't know why this resonates with me so deeply, except that it seems to echo grace. There is, in the waiting, acceptance.

These are the words, the message I preach to myself today:

I wish I had known I was capable of making good decisions.

There was always someone willing, too willing, to speak for me, to turn my head. There were too many voices saying they

Anna White

spoke for God.

I wish I had known I could hear and taste and see for myself, because when I left the voices behind, I was lost. How do you know who you are when everything that defined you is gone? How do you even know how to speak?

I had to build a new foundation, start from the ground up.

If your voice is lost today, sit still and quiet. Be with the uneasiness that rises up. Don't go looking for another voice to speak God to you. Just sit and wait. Let the restlessness rise and the shadows fall.

There is too much talk. Too much chatter and opinion and fence-making. The noise is deafening, but the Voice isn't in the noise.

Stay and listen into the silence.

Sometimes love is good enough to make us wait.

Mended

"My sun sets to rise again."
    Robert Browning

Anna White

THOUGHTS ON STAYING AFTER ELEVEN YEARS TOGETHER

I have been reading <u>Tiny Beautiful Things</u> by Cheryl Strayed. She's an online advice columnist, and the book is a collection of letters from her readers and her letters back to them. I believe she is very wise and mostly right, even if she does curse more than anyone I know.

Towards the end of the book Cheryl, aka Sugar, shares three letters from women who are thinking about leaving their husbands. She puts these letters together, because she believes that together they tell a complete picture. In her answer, Sugar describes her own first marriage, and how she made the decision to leave it for no definable reason except that she felt she must.

"Go!" she encourages the letter writers. "Go!"

Here, I must disagree with Sugar. I got married when I was 20, to a lovely normal man. He was many things that I was not, including mature and emotionally stable. Before the wedding, and immediately after, my mind shouted at me to RUN RUN RUN! I sweated through the nights and cried through the days because every twitching fiber of my being wanted me to go, but there was one small corner of logical thought that kept talking me down.

There are lots of real reasons to decide to leave something or someone, but there are lots of other reasons that are less valid and less real and less about a relationship than our own minds: Fear (of screwing up, of being left, of not being good enough), restlessness, resistance to growing up, PMS, not knowing how to live without drama, fearing that you're getting happy, and happiness is boring.

The thing that scared me the most was the knowledge that if I stayed, something was going to change, and that something was probably me. I didn't know what changed me would look like, or if I would like her more or less than I already did. Would I still recognize myself? Would I still *be* myself?

None of these were good reasons for going, because if the reason is my own crazymaking self, then, as the saying goes, "Wherever I go, there I am." I will find myself and my crazymaking ways thinking exactly the same things a month or six months or a year later and have the same choice to make again. Stay or Go?

I could be going forever, which at some point looks a lot

like running away.

He had reasons to go too. Getting married to a beautiful depressed person who, while not exactly in love with someone else is not entirely over them either, seemed like a big mistake. He told me later that being married was so horribly different than he expected he wondered if he had ruined his life.

And yet, here we are. Neither of us chose to go, and somewhere along the way we learned to love each other well. The past eleven years have brought us happiness and suffering, but these have not defined us. We have chosen to fall together and not apart.

I am thankful for the years, and for the examples we have in a long marriage. Not only my parents and his, but also our grandparents and aunts and uncles. This is rare in the world today, but beautiful. I am fortunate to be surrounded by living pictures of what it looks like to stay.

I can't say for sure if I'm better off, since I have no way of knowing what would have been. I could have traveled to exotic places and kissed exotic men in the moonlight. Or I could have ended up living alone in a dumpy apartment with the flesh eating virus I contracted from a public toilet. Could haves are always a great unknown.

Society tells us leaving is the stuff, exciting and daring and fresh. Sometimes it is. But it is staying that goes deep and carves

Mended

Grand Canyons out of the plains of our lives. The waters run and run and run, and they are always the same and somehow always different. We lose parts of ourselves to the staying, get rounder and smoother, and in spite of all that we have lost, bigger too. Each season turns and flows past, every experience leading to the same place: to the end, and then out into the deep wide sea.

Anna White

"Dance when you're broken open.
Dance if you've torn the bandage off.
Dance in the middle of fighting.
Dance in your blood.
Dance when you're perfectly free."
Rumi

Mended

BURN

We had an unplanned fire drill last week. We were standing around in front of the school when the secretary teased, "Why'd you grab your purse? I know you don't have any money in there."

"My journals are in there," I said.

She thought this was funny, but to me my journals are valuable because I'm a writer.

Can I say that? I don't have an editor or an agent. I'm not published or famous or viral, but I write.

I have a friend, an artist, that doesn't want to call himself an artist because he thinks it sounds pompous. "I had classes with *artists*," he said. "I didn't like them."

"But you are an artist," I said. "You love art. You see art. You make art. You're an artist. Just don't be a pompous jerk artist."

Why is it so hard to claim the parts of ourselves that lie the deepest? Is it because we're afraid of what it would mean or because they feel bigger than we are?

Writer, musician, artist, poet, chef, whatever the name of the little coal that burns within you, the title seems to hold a weight and a meaning. We feel like we need recognition and pay and affirmation before we can pick it up, or for someone else to bestow the title onto us.

I don't believe those things are necessary. I think it's enough to find, deep in our own soul, that we are already who we long to be. We are what we do in our own silence.

You have permission to name yourself, to claim your own identity. This isn't a pompous action, but a prophetic, life-affirming truth. Speak it. Whisper it five times fast.

I am a _____,

Say it until you believe it's true.

Let all your thoughts and ideas run free. Let them pour out and turn them around carefully to assess their worth. Ask each thought, *What do you want from me? Do you have a place here?* Decide if it's a thought to let run across your palms and through your fingers, a thought to hold onto, to file away, or a dream to bury, in hope that it will sprout into some larger thing. Do not judge, sweet dreamer. Do not close your heart away.

Let your flame burn. Be a light in the darkness. A candle

Mended

can give away light to ten or a hundred or a thousand other candles, but the sharing doesn't shadow the light. The flame keeps burning brightly. It is the act of passing the spark on that magnifies us and makes the whole world brighter.

Anna White

"May what I do flow from me like a river,
no forcing and no holding back."
  Rilke

Mended

MOTHERS

The rhythm of life is in the patterns. It is the meaning beneath the busy, the steadiness that keeps us moving when our legs are shaking and our muscles are begging for rest.

It is a dance, the things we do.

I wake up every morning to the patter of running feet ending in a THUMP at my bedroom door. Then comes the high cry for toast, juice, PBS kids. The dance begins.

The day is all step, all movement. I bend and twirl and wipe and clean. I walk the paths from living room to kitchen to bathroom and back. I search for the same things every day. Where are the keys? The wipes? The remote? Where is that missing puzzle piece?

My husband teases me because I search for the same channels, every time. I never learn the numbers. I ignore the dust behind the couch and the crumbs that are (always) on the table. I choose what to see and what to not see.

I close my eyes and try to hear, beyond the squeals and the

grind of the garbage disposal, the music. It is up to me to bring grace into the dance, to let myself be spun laughing into the arms of busy.

Months ago I sat across from a mother who was getting back custody of her children for the first time in years. She told me how nervous she was about their first night together, how she wanted everything to be "right."

"I've been on the bottom," she said. "I woke up one day and I realized I'm going to live, or I'm going to die, but I cannot live like this."

"I've been there," I said. My bottom was different than yours, but I've had to choose between living and dying too. It hasn't been so long ago that I sat down in the middle of my life and said 'I am done. Help me or carry me or drag me, because I cannot take one more step.'"

I think this is what we all want to hear: that we are not alone in hitting the bottom, and that it is possible to come out of that place courageous, beautiful, and strong.

We talked about the responsibility of caring for little lives, and our mother-heart desire to keep them from falling. "I'll go in the streets after them," she said. "I'm with them 'til the end."

I laughed and said our children will probably go down completely different roads than the ones we've learned to

Mended

navigate. We talked about the desire to reach perfection, and how we can never quite touch that shining star. I spoke about the grace that we must gift to others, and especially ourselves-the grace to fail and try again.

When she left, I hugged her. We were strangers that saw each other, just for a moment. We were sharing the same struggle to live down the hours and days and minutes with realness and purpose and heart.

We were both just learning to dance.

Anna White

"You can have the other words-chance, luck, coincidence, serendipity. I'll take grace. I don't know what it is exactly, but I'll take it."
Mary Oliver

Mended

BEGINNING OF THE END

December is finally here. Advent. The season of waiting. The beginning of the end.

This year has been a year of change for me. This year I turned 30. I laid things to rest. This year, I decided to rise.

I remember getting up January first and sitting in my chair, desperate for God. What I wanted Him to do for me I couldn't say, but I got up and sat there every day. My own season of waiting. My personal advent.

Tonight my daughter and I sit on the balcony of our hotel room and listen to the waves in the Gulf of Mexico. We could see it earlier, but it's dark now.

"I love it out here," she says. She tucks her bare feet beneath her nightgown until only her toes stick out. "I can see *everything*." A lady comes out to walk her dog and my daughter waves down at her.

Then she points her finger up into the night sky. "There's a bright star," she says. "I wonder if it will lead us to baby Jesus."

Anna White

"I don't know," I say. "It might."

She thinks about this. "I want to give baby Jesus one of my dollies, Baby TeeWee with the brown hair."

I'm surprised by this declaration. I know how she loves her dollies, her babies. "Are you sure?"

"The Wise Men brought gifts," she says, "and the shepherd that came later gave his little lamb." She stops, as if this explains everything. I guess it does.

"Ok," I say. I nod into the dark. "If you gave Jesus a dolly, I think He would like that."

She nods and wrinkles her nose. "Yeah," she says. "I think he would."

Mended

"It is better to light a single candle
than to curse the darkness."
Peter Beneson

Anna White

LIGHT A CANDLE AGAINST THE DARK

This week all four of us are sick in one way or another, and so my sleep schedule is off. I've been blessed by my friends this week, old and new, but those are stories for another day. All I can say now is that I have laughed and laughed and laughed.

In this week I see such a picture of life, hard and joyful pressed up together and sleeping in the same bed. They come knit together. The lines of pain run through the joy and remind us to go all in, because life is short. The joy edges the pain and gives us a reason to rise.

I'm just coming home from a night out with friends. It's cold outside, one of the first nights that feels like fall, but I feel warm. I sit at my paint splattered desk nesting, Adele on the radio, a stack of books beside me. I hold a space for the evening. I light a candle.

My husband and I were in Westminster Abbey on my 25th birthday. The trip to London was really for him, a lifelong dream. We were tense, angry, strung out from jet lag and navigating the city with pocket maps, but there, in the Abbey,

Mended

we heard the organ play.

I stood beneath the sweeping arches that have sheltered so many and withstood wars and bombs and weddings and funerals. The slabs of stone, worn by the feet of so many pilgrims, just continue to stand. I imagined the songs that had been sung here, the prayers that had been prayed. How many?

On our way out my husband stopped and lit a candle for me, on my birthday. He held my hand there in the back of the church and prayed a blessing over me, thanking God for the gift of my life and for the years to come.

This is what I think about tonight as I look at the candle flickering beside me: prayers and blessing. I light my candle and I wait. I make my peace.

I took my oldest daughter for a moonwalk. She and I are the least sick of the four, so I made hot chocolate and bundled her up in our red Radio Flyer wagon and down the street we went. We couldn't see the moon, but we looked at Christmas lights and the stars.

The only sounds we heard were one barking dog, the wagon wheels against the road, and the hush of car wheels flying across the interstate in the distance. As we walked she leaned back and looked up into the sky, and we talked about the stars. I told her that the Bible says the stars show us the wonder of God, because people make many things beautiful, like the decorated houses we were passing, but no person could hang all those stars. There are just too many, too far away.

"Sometimes," I said, "I wonder if there is anything out there, or if we are all alone. But when I look at the stars, I see something bigger than myself. The stars help me choose to believe."

Matthew Henry says, "The heavens so declare the glory of God, and proclaim his wisdom, power, and goodness, that all are left without excuse. They speak themselves to be works of God's hands; for they must have a Creator who is eternal, infinitely wise, powerful, and good."

Yes, I choose to believe.

Mended

"I will not live an unlived life.
I will not live in fear of falling or catching fire.
I choose to inhabit my days."
Dawn Markova

Anna White

STRUGGLE

I am struggling this morning, which is really code for 'burning down in flames.' Every time I feel this way I think, *Be ignited or be gone.*

The winter cold and rain has blown in strong, and when I look out my window I see dim light and shades of gray. When I look inward, I feel gray too. These are the times when I wonder, *Is it just me? Or do we all have a bare soul winter?*

I've been dwelling a little on where I was last month. I had a good thing going, felt totally centered, dropped down deep into the core of my life. I felt holy, calling on holy, walking on holy.

The only thing that's changed is me. I choose to believe what was calling is calling still. This is the test of all things: to continue when your head is quiet and your heart is still. To get up anyway and sit in the chair anyway, pulling your heart through the dust behind you. To do the work when it feels like work.

It's not a war: me vs depression. A war implies an end, a

Mended

victor, one side firebombing the other into oblivion. There can be no firebombing, no obliteration, when all the fighting is inside of me. I will not go down, I will not turn to ash, but I cannot destroy the flames. I beat them back and they just keep on rising, spreading, and jumping the ring of bare earth I'm trying to scratch out.

I'm more comfortable with the idea of things as a struggle. I think of Jacob wrestling with the angel. I can feel it, fingers digging into the side of the stranger, pressed up against one another, bones breaking, rocks bruising into skin as we roll on the ground and get more and more covered with dirt. Holding on. Not letting go. Demanding, "Bless me. Bless me and change my name."

Maybe it's love that's holding us down.

I came across this poem a few days ago, and although it is very old it seems like the truest thing I have read in a long time. If you're burning today, read this slowly.

Don't let go.

> Love wants to reach out and manhandle us.
>
> Break up all our teacup talk of God.
>
> If you had the courage and

Anna White

> could give the Beloved his choice, some nights
> He would just drag you around the room
> by your hair,
> ripping from your grip all those toys in the world
> that bring you joy.
>
> Love sometimes gets tired of speaking sweetly
> and wants to rip to shreds
> all your erroneous notions of truth
> that make you fight within yourself, dear one,
> and with others.
> Causing the world to weep
> on too many fine days.
>
> God wants to manhandle us,
> lock us inside of a tiny room with Himself
> and practice His dropkick.
> The Beloved sometimes wants

Mended

to do us a great favor:

hold us upside down

and shake all the nonsense out.

But when we hear

He is in such a "playful drunken mood"

most everyone I know

quickly packs their bags and hightails it

out of town.

"Tired of Speaking Sweetly"

From <u>The Gift</u> by Hafiz

Translated by Daniel Ladinsky

Anna White

"You are helpful and you are loved
and you are forgiven and you are not alone."
John Green

Mended

THANK YOU FOR YOUR GIFT

One of my friends told me a story about Mother Teresa. She entered a bakery with a street child to ask for bread, and the baker spit in her face. Mother Teresa simply said, "Thank you for your gift. Now perhaps something for the child."

This is all I've been thinking. "Thank you for your gift." Because every experience, every feeling is a gift. They all have something to teach me.

Yesterday I had bone deep shivers. I sat at my desk and tried to work, and inside I was thinking, *the fall, the fall, the fall.* I saw it coming like a tornado on the horizon, throwing cows and roaring like a freight train.

And yet, it was not so bad. I didn't fight it. I didn't list ten reasons why I *shouldn't* have bone deep shivers. I whispered to myself, *I am and they are. Thank you for your gift.*

I tap my fingers on my desk. I breathe in calm. I breathe out fear. I run my thumb over the cool ridges of my water glass. I breathe in still. I breathe out rush. The last time I felt this way

Anna White

I ended up being offered Prozac by the new midwife. Today I stopped at Walgreens on the way home and bought wrapping paper and tape.

We watched part of <u>Elf</u>. We made paper snowflakes and threw the paper scraps up in the air and yelled, "Snow!" over and over again, because that's all the snow there is. Oldest and I wrapped presents for Daddy. She taped them and put them under the tree, and then promptly showed him each one.

"There's your game, Daddy," she said. "There's your book." No amount of shushing could subdue her voice. Thank you for your gift.

I went to bed early, my eyes heavy with tornado dust, but my heart quiet.

I fall, again, I rise.

Thank you for your gift.

Mended

"I loved you at your darkest."
Romans 5:8

Anna White

THIN PLACES

Last week I read about thin places. These are places believed to be spiritual, where it is a bit easier to touch the divine. In thin places "heaven kisses earth, and eternal time brushes against ordinary time."

There are sites, map coordinates for these locations. We could go there, you and I. We could make a pilgrimage and sit cross legged under the vast blue sky. They say, people that know, that God hovers close there.

What I want, through this holiday season and forever, is for my heart to be the thin place. I don't want to board a plane to feel the kiss of heaven. I want to carry it with me wherever I go. I want my fragile, hurting heart, to recognize fleeting kairos, eternal moments, as they pass. I want to be my own mountain and my own retreat.

After I finish this post, I'm taking the rest of the week off from writing. Family is coming to visit. There will be meals prepared together, candles lit, hands held. There will be a resting together.

Mended

I love you too. You have encouraged me in so many moments. Your words and emails held me when I was drifting through the dark. I am sitting here by the fire, cozy in body and soul. I am thinking of you and saying a prayer. May your heart be thin. May the eternal kiss you.

Anna White

"Let life get to you. And be truly moved by the awesome wonder of it all."
Ralph Marston

Mended

TO A SISTER AT CHRISTMAS

Dear Sister,

I heard you are worn thin this holiday season, separated from family that you hold dear.

Christmas is such a time of struggle anyway, crammed with busy and hurry and the expectation that you will be joyful, no matter what. Then, if you're like me, when you just sit quietly, just be, and let yourself feel what you feel, the guilt creeps in. Because you're alive and the world is big, and you *should* be feeling some freakin' Christmas spirit.

Well I'll tell you sister, that it's okay to not feel it. It's okay if seeing Santa makes you sad, and the endless carols give you a headache, and the aisles of candy canes make you want to stay out of the grocery store. It's okay.

I don't know what your faith is, or if you believe in truth, or if God speaks to you. This is what has been speaking to me lately. In Daniel 3, the Hebrew boys prayed the hardest prayer. The prayer birthed out of the knowledge of suffering.

Anna White

The God we serve is able to save us...but even if He does not we still will not serve your gods. Daniel 3:18

This is life. The God I serve is able to save us both. To give us the winning lottery ticket so all our money problems will go away. To mend our broken hearts. To bring us close to those we love. He is able. He is able. He is able.

But even if He doesn't, do not bow to bitterness. Do not fall down onto your broken pieces and let them cut you to ribbons. Even if He doesn't do all that He is able to do, all that we wish He would do, He is good.

Sometimes His goodness is just higher than our eyes can see.

I pray that you find peace in this season. That you find rest and relief, and most of all that you remain able to see His goodness. Even if.

Mended

"Our job is to love others without stopping to inquire whether or not they are worthy."
Thomas Merton

Anna White

THE THICK DARKNESS WHERE GOD WAS (THE DAY OF THE SANDY HOOK SHOOTING)

Today I search for words to write. I have to write, because this is how I shape my world, and yet what grieves me seems unshapeable, senseless suffering and pain and darkness. What I want to do is hunker down until I know the names of the precious souls brutally ripped from this world. I want to write their names on my arms in Sharpie, hard black lines for honor and for memory.

It seems to me that it is the random acts of violence that hurt the most, because no matter where these acts occur, they reach into each of our lives and chip away at our sense of safety. The grief feels near, like it is mine. In this moment, I struggle to understand God.

Because I believe, that He is in all things, even this. I believe He was there, with the children lost, with the survivors scarred, with the families broken. Even, in the end, with the shooter. It is unthinkable to me. All I see is one horrible act, a regrettable life. If the shooter was wiped from all records, his body burned

Mended

and scattered with no grave or tombstone, it would not be enough for me. And yet even he had a soul.

In Exodus the Bible says Moses drew near to the thick darkness where God was. I must believe He is there still, in this thick darkness, so deep and black and senseless. And so I pray:

Father, be near as we are surrounded by this cloud of deep suffering. Open our eyes to see that you are all things, the light and the darkness, not only those things that seem good in our eyes, but the horrifying unexplainable. Wrap us up inside of the cloud and reveal the mysteries that can only be learned in places of sorrow, that when we walk out we will be as Moses, transformed by the shadow and beaming with the radiant light of your glory. Give us the strength to love on, though our hearts are broken.

Anna White

"I have decided to stick with love.
Hate is too great a burden to bear."
Martin Luther King Jr.

SURRENDER

I opened Facebook yesterday and saw a picture of two grim looking white kids with their hands wrapped around weapons taller than they were. "Why Assault Rifles?" screamed the caption.

And I'm still stuck on the first word. I can't get any farther than that.

Why?

I grew up singing about how we are soldiers in God's army. Six years old, we shaped our fingers into guns and spun around firing at the invisible. I'm older now: old enough to have wrapped my fingers around the cold metal of a pistol, old enough to have stared down a barrel and pulled a trigger, old enough to know I don't want to fight.

I don't want to see life as a battle.

I believe in beauty. I believe in goodness. I believe in the power of turning: the other cheek, time, curve of the earth.

Anna White

And yet, the battle finds me.

I fight the steady tug of the dark. I fight small. I fight tired doubt and chest-clenching anxiety and cynicism and fear of the future. I fight it all.

I step daily onto my battlefield, and I see Quiet, Enough, Faith, Community off in the distance. I push forward, trying to protect my only heart, and as I clash against harsh words and judgment and expectations, I think, *Armor on? Armor off?*

What if I fear no evil?

What if I lay my weapons down?

What if I let all that fear run right through me?

The anticipation of the pain might be worse than the wound itself. It might be that the blood and tears will form a river that will carry me out of the dust and the explosions and the screaming. They might form a river that will carry me to myself.

I imagine myself floating down that crimson thread, a white flag of surrender lying over my eyes. Dying to what I know. What I want. What I dream.

All surrender, swept along in a flow of love-grace, until I come to rest in that distant place my soul desires.

Mended

"Love is the whole thing. We are only pieces."
Rumi

Anna White

FOREBODING JOY 2

I was driving to work thinking about how gloriously happy I was. It reminded me of the day my husband and I were on a dingy sidewalk in California and I smelled the most wonderful smell. I followed it, my nose twitching like a Spaniel's, into this little hole in the wall ice cream shop where they were making homemade waffle cones. Right there! It was amazing! I think it was the happiest moment of my life.

I don't say this to discount all the other amazing and much more significant moments in my life: the day the preacher said, "You may kiss the bride", when my water broke three weeks early, seeing my daughters' faces as we approached Cinderella's castle for the first time. Those moments were bigger and more expensive and life changing and planned. There was too much anticipation and expectation wrapped up in them to be totally free.

Discovering the waffle cones, that was a totally unexpected, unweighted moment. That type of happiness is the best.

So today I'm driving to work, thinking about how happy I

Mended

feel and how wonderful it is to be alive and have leopard shoes and spangley scarves to put on and about wrapping Christmas presents tonight and just all the goodness in the whole freaking world, and then about two minutes later I realize that I am thinking about what I would do if I got to work and found out that my husband was in a car accident on *his* way to work and he and my girls were killed.

When I caught myself, I was imagining sitting at their wake, and wondering if it would be worth paying my counselor by the hour to come sit with me and help me deal with my grief. Curse that foreboding joy!

As soon as I realized what was happening I told myself, "Hey! Back to the reveling at the birds and blades of grass. The sun is rising, no one is dying-cut it out!" And I did.

I doubt it ever goes away, foreboding joy, not as long as we still have something to live for. But recognizing it and calling it out, for today that was enough.

Anna White

"Something very beautiful happens to people when their world has fallen apart: a humility, a nobility, a higher intelligence emerges at just the pony when our knees hit the floor."
Marianne Williamson

Mended

HELLO HURRICANE

I met a friend for coffee this morning. We sat beside the water just after sunrise eating sweetbreads and watching the birds dive down.

Where I live, 30 miles from the Gulf, hurricanes are just a part of life. Storm trackers are free at Popeye's and we stock up on bottled water. Sometimes the storms run us North and send us seeking shelter, but often we stay. We board up, stock up, lock up, and show the storm a healthy measure of respect.

What we know, those of us that live near the water, is that if the storm comes we will pull together to repair what's windblown broken. We know that after the storm, God shows up. We see how strong we are, what a community we have, and how many people love us.

It hasn't been so many years since this place I sit now with my friend, my favorite place, was underwater. It was an empty lot before the hurricane came and everything within a mile of the lake flooded. It was in the aftermath that the beautifully unexpected grew. The lot was transformed into a gorgeous park that is filled every day with flowers and fountains and dogs and children.

This weekend, if the hurricane is rolling in, winds raging and sky turning dark, throw open your arms. Let the storm blow around you. Let the rain pour down. No matter how fierce the hurricane may be, it can't take your love. You are enough. Your love is strong enough. You will make it through. The flood may reveal an opportunity to transform into something even more beautiful.

Mended

"I decided that the most subversive, revolutionary thing I could do was to show up for my life and not be ashamed."
Anne Lamott

Anna White

SHUTTING UP MY MONKEY MIND

My mind whips into high gear as soon as I get an idea. "Make a plan!" it urges. "Figure out what you're going to do. Make a day by day chart. Get organized."

The Buddhists call this busy grasping at nothing the 'monkey mind'. My monkey mind has been jumping and screaming for my attention for weeks. I'm trying to ignore it, or at least throw a few nuts through the bars to shut it up, but old habits die hard.

Truth: last week I online shopped too much. Then I ate 2 pounds of jelly beans to feel better about that. In fact, while I was trying to read soul-nourishing things all I could think about was shopping and jellybeans. Points to the monkey mind.

The challenge is to stare it all down, the thoughts and my failures, and start again. So today, when all those ideas started popping like kernels in a hot skillet I said, "Mind, I *hear* you loud and clear, but NO THANK YOU! Today is all I can handle. I choose to stick with that."

Mended

And what was today? A collection of moments hung together by quiet spaces. A conversation about how to encourage our daughter. Cooking, feeding the baby, opening packages (compliments of the aforementioned shopping). Ignoring the towel mountain in the corner of my bedroom. Cookies in the oven. Music playing through the house.

Enough.

I've decided to give my monkey mind a name, because he's alive and well each morning. He tells me I shouldn't write because I'm going to run out of things to say soon, and then I will be an empty failure. That I have nothing new to add to the discussion, nothing new to give. That I should delete all my old blog posts to hide evidence of my stopping and starting.

He's like a pet nipping around my heels, not powerful, but annoying. I choose to hear his chattering words and shine a light right into his beady little eyes. I want him to know that I see him in all his ugly smallness.

After giving it some thought, I've decided to name my monkey mind Ricky Bobby. I was thinking about Latin names like Javier, but I don't want to make my jumping, distractable self sound mysterious and sexy. Ricky Bobby makes me laugh. A name like that seems silly, not strong. Just a goofy little thing that doesn't know what to do with his hands, likes to go fast, and loves tiny, infant, baby Jesus. I can live with that.

Anna White

Seeing my mind this way allows me to be a little more tolerant, a little more forgiving. I can say to Ricky Bobby, as Elizabeth Gilbert does to her monkey mind in <u>Eat, Pray, Love</u>, "Run out and play. Mommy's talking to God."

Mended

"One of the most calming and powerful actions you can do in a stormy world is to stand up and show your soul."
Clarissa Pinkola Estes

Anna White

SHINING ALL THE WAY DOWN

The alarm went off this morning, and I couldn't get out of bed. My husband came in and found me still under the covers. He bent over and kissed my forehead and said, "You are so loved."

I could barely stand it, because I am falling heavy. I feel sorry for him and for my daughters, because they are so whole and good, and I am just a hot mess. I hide out in the shower while they get ready, and then feel even more ashamed for avoiding them, these beautiful gifts that live in my house.

On the way to work I drive across a canal and the fog is lying heavy over the surface of the water. That's me, I think. They are cloud, and I am low-lying fog.

Anne Lamott writes in her book Help, Thanks, Wow about the glorious surprise of this. We wonder how we ever got so lucky to have such wise and lovely people around us, who tolerate us in all of our screwed up broken mess. And somehow, beyond reason, they feel the same way about us, also wondering how they got so lucky. This is truest love, when each person

Mended

feels that are getting the better deal.

This is the great mystery.

Last night we went out walking, bundled up against the dark. The girls rode in the wagon with our dog and we walked alongside. The stars were bright, and we tried to map out their shapes with our fingers. My daughter says there's a bunny in the moon, but tonight we couldn't find it; it was hiding somewhere out of sight. Maybe it was sinking too, falling below the horizon. Even falling it keeps on shining, all the way down.

Anna White

"The first question I ask when something doesn't seem to be beautiful is why do I think it's not beautiful? And very shortly you discover that there is no reason."
John Cage

Mended

WHAT I WANT MY KIDS TO KNOW

You are, and always will be, loved, no matter who you become or what choices you make. You deserve love. You will always have worth, because you are a precious soul.

Does this mean there will be no hard consequences? No. But I promise I will not degrade you. I will not say, "I told you so." I will stand by you, because you are my child. I will always be in your corner.

I will love you, because all of us are worthy of love. I will forgive you, because I have walked in darkness and needed forgiveness. We all fall. We all fail. These moments are not what define you. What matters most is how you rise.

When I first wrote this into my journal, I planned to print it to go in my daughters' rooms. I talk to them already about worthiness, about relationship, and about love that exists outside of their behavior.

One memorable day we were walking home from the park,

and child 1 was screaming and crying *very* loudly and dramatically. I told her in my quiet teacher voice that although her behavior was not very good at the moment, *she* was good and I loved her. She was still a precious soul.

She started screaming, "I don't love you! YOU ARE NOT PRECIOUS!"

We did this all the way home, me saying things like, "I hear that you are angry. This is not acceptable behavior. But I still love you," and her screaming, **"NOOOOO! I don't love you! I DO NOT LOVE YOU!"**

My mom says she is too young to understand when I say these things to her, and maybe that's true, but who knows the magic age? I don't know at what point she will understand, and I want these truths, You are worthy, You are loved, You are a precious soul, to be the first things that she remembers.

Not getting pushed off the slide at school. Not making me proud for doing something well. Not learning to write her name. Not the arrival of her sister. Not how to make me smile.

All those things matter, but they are not what I want to be first. When she is my age and doubt and insecurity and fear slip into her bed, I want the deepest, farthest back thing, the words pressed right up against her heart, to be *Worthy, Loved, Precious*. Even if I'm no longer able to say it. Even if no one else says it.

This is a message for all of us. No matter how old we are,

Mended

no matter what our deepest words are, this is what the Father whispers: You too are worthy. You too are loved. You too are precious. Without condition.

Anna White

"May today there be peace within.
May you trust God that you are exactly where you are meant to be.
May you not forget the infinite possibilities that are born of faith.
May you use those gifts that you have received, and pass on the love that has been given to you.
May you be content knowing you are a child of God.
Let this presence settle into your bones, and allow your soul the freedom to sing, dance, praise, and love."

Therese de Lisieux

Mended

NOTES

I referenced the following authors, musicians, and movies in the book. They inspire my heart and I encourage you to consider this a list for dark days:

Brene Brown, *Daring Greatly* (Gotham, 2012)
Emily Freeman, *Grace for the Good Girl* (Revell, 2011)
Elizabeth Gilbert, *Eat, Pray, Love* (Penguin, 2006)
Hafiz and Daniel Ladinsky, *The Gift* (Penguin, 1999)
Matthew Henry, *Whole Bible Commentary* (Nelson, 2002)
Anne Lamott, *Help, Thanks, Wow* (Penguin, 2013)
Glennon Melton, *Carry on Warrior* (Scribner, 2013)
Mary Oliver, *New and Selected Poems v. 1* (Beacon Press, 2004)
Phillip Phillips, *Home* (Interscope Records, 2012)
Rainer Marie Rilke, *Letters to a Young Poet* (Merchant Books, 2012)
J.K. Rowling, *Harry Potter and the Order of the Phoenix* (Arthur A. Levine Books, 2003)
Cheryl Strayed, *Tiny Beautiful Things* (Vintage, 2012)
Switchfoot, *Hello Hurricane* (Atlantic, 2009)
Talladega Nights: The Ballad of Ricky Bobby (Sony Pictures, 2006)
Ann Voskamp, *1000 Gifts* (Zondervan, 2011)

Anna White

I AM THANKFUL

For my husband, who tolerates my need for silence and gives me time to write.

For my children, who make me laugh and remind me what it looks like to live free of self-consciousness and fear.

For all my sister friends, in real life and online, who have encouraged me on and shared their stories with me. You remind me that I am not alone.

For my parents, who always give me love and support, even when they don't understand what in the world I'm doing.

For my inspiring art teachers and the other writers who put their heart on display every single day. They make me bold, they make me brave, and they show me how to walk the hard path.

For God, who is daily teaching me to see through His eyes.

For my readers, especially those who have sent me personal messages of encouragement through the years. They always come at just the right moment. Thank you for taking the journey with me.

Did you enjoy Mended?

I'd love it if you left a review on Amazon!
Add the link to your review to the form at

www.eepurl.com/ODBPX

and you'll get a free copy of
Soul Rest: Retreating to the Heart of Life
as a thank you.

Made in United States
North Haven, CT
02 January 2023